Digging Deeper into the Past

The Egyptians

John and Louise James

ACKNOWLEDGEMENTS

First published in Great Britain in 1998
by Heinemann Library,
Halley Court, Jordan Hill, Oxford, OX2 8EJ,
a division of Reed Educational & Professional Publishing Ltd.

OXFORD MELBOURNE AUCKLAND
JOHANNESBURG BLANTYRE GABORONE
IBADAN PORTSMOUTH (NH) USA CHICAGO

Written by: Louise James **Illustrated by**: John James
Editor: Andrew Farrow **Design**: John James and Joanna Malivoire

02 01 00 99 98
10 9 8 7 6 5 4 3 2 1

ISBN 0 431 07174 8

British Library Cataloguing in Publication Data
James, John
The Egyptians. - (Digging deeper into the past)
1.Egypt - civilization - Juvenile literature 2.Egypt -
History - To 640 A.D. - Juvenile literature
I.Title II.James, Louise
932

This title is also available in a hardback library edition (ISBN 0 431 0717 2).
Printed and bound in Italy

The publishers would like to thank Delia Pemberton for her advice and assistance in the preparation of this book,
and the organizations that have given their permission to reproduce the following pictures:

AKG Photo, London: 14 (relief), 15 (relief).
Ancient Art and Architecture Collection: 29 (vulture and funeral mask).
Bexhill Museum/Reg Hawkins: 12 (mouse and spinning top).
Courtesy of the Trustees of the British Museum: 6 (Rosetta stone, tomb painting, papyrus), 7 (X-rays), 9 (necklace),
10 (mummified calf), 14 (boat, right), 17 (fish flask and hippopotamus), 21 (wall painting and limestone flake),
18 (Bes figure), 19 (kneeling priest), 23 (register), 24 (ostracon), 25 (papyrus).
Fitzwilliam Museum: 12 (doll), 21 (spoon). **Florence Museum**: 25 (scribes).
Hildesheim Museum: 28 (Anubis mask).
Jurgen Liepe: 8 (table and game), 18 (bracelet), 20 (porter), 26 (spearmen), 27 (prisoners of war).
Michael Holford: 10 (tomb model), 11 (baker), 23 (papyrus plans), 29 (statue).
Museo Egizio, Turin: 9 (cosmetic box).
Museum of Fine Arts, Boston: 6 (mummy's head), 22 (ration tokens).
Peter Clayton: 16 (fishing boats).
Robert Harding Picture Library: 14 (Tutankhamun's boat), 26 (daggers), 29 (statue).
States Museum, Berlin: 20 (doctor's case).
Werner Forman Archive: 11 (person cooking).

Every effort has been made to contact copyright holders of any material reproduced in this book.
Any omissions will be rectified in subsequent printings if notice is given to the Publisher.

CONTENTS

 SETTING THE SCENE 4

 HISTORY IN EVIDENCE 6

 A WEALTHY FAMILY 8

 FARMING 10

 A WORKER'S HOUSE 12

 TRADE 14

 HUNTING AND FISHING 16

 PROCESSION OF THE GOD 18

 LIFE AT THE TEMPLE 20

 MOVING A COLOSSUS 22

 SCRIBES 24

 WARFARE 26

 THE TOMB OF TUTANKHAMUN 28

 GLOSSARY 30

 INDEX 32

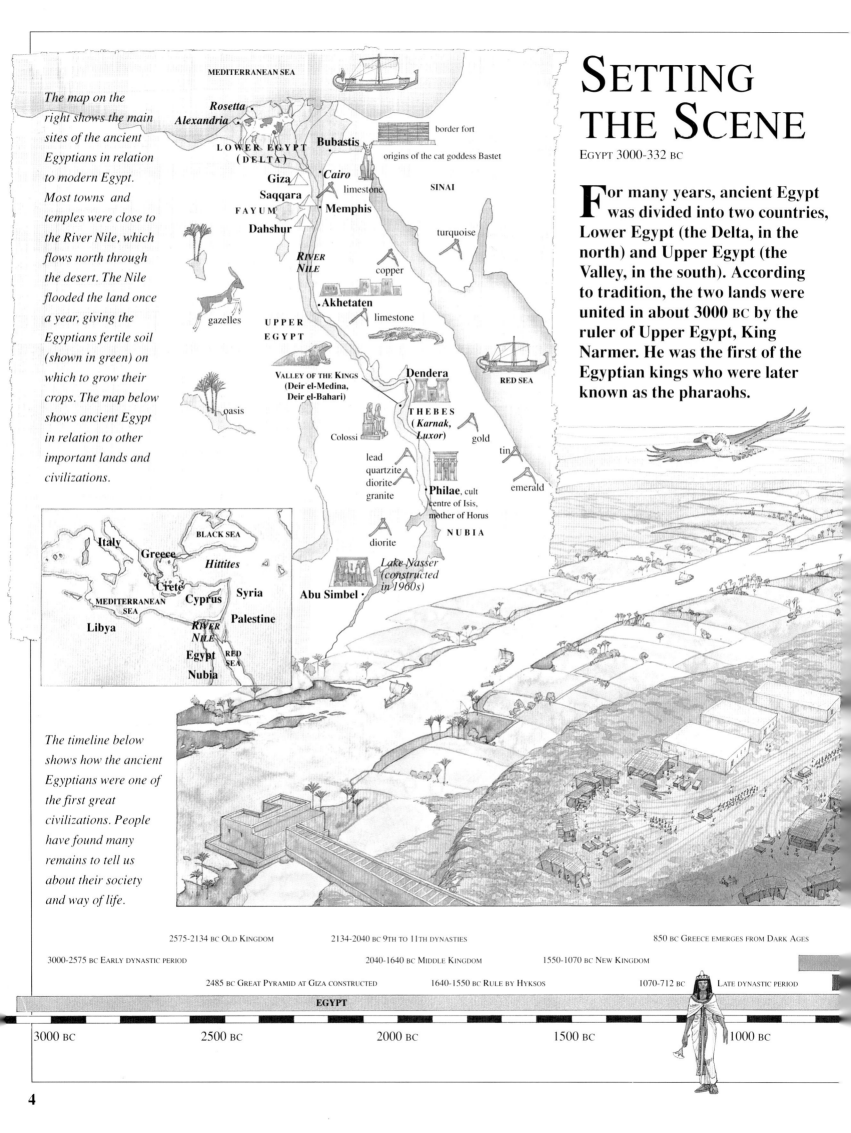

SETTING THE SCENE

EGYPT 3000-332 BC

The map on the right shows the main sites of the ancient Egyptians in relation to modern Egypt. Most towns and temples were close to the River Nile, which flows north through the desert. The Nile flooded the land once a year, giving the Egyptians fertile soil (shown in green) on which to grow their crops. The map below shows ancient Egypt in relation to other important lands and civilizations.

For many years, ancient Egypt was divided into two countries, Lower Egypt (the Delta, in the north) and Upper Egypt (the Valley, in the south). According to tradition, the two lands were united in about 3000 BC by the ruler of Upper Egypt, King Narmer. He was the first of the Egyptian kings who were later known as the pharaohs.

The timeline below shows how the ancient Egyptians were one of the first great civilizations. People have found many remains to tell us about their society and way of life.

MEDITERRANEAN SEA

Rosetta
Alexandria
LOWER EGYPT (DELTA)
Bubastis
border fort
origins of the cat goddess Bastet
Cairo
Giza
limestone
SINAI
Saqqara
FAYUM
Memphis
Dahshur
turquoise
RIVER NILE
copper
gazelles
Akhetaten
limestone
UPPER EGYPT
oasis
VALLEY OF THE KINGS
(Deir el-Medina, Deir el-Bahari)
Dendera
RED SEA
THEBES (Karnak, Luxor)
Colossi
gold
tin
lead
quartzite
diorite
granite
Philae, cult centre of Isis, mother of Horus
emerald
NUBIA
diorite
Lake Nasser (constructed in 1960s)
Abu Simbel

Italy
BLACK SEA
Greece
Hittites
Crete
Cyprus
Syria
MEDITERRANEAN SEA
Libya
Palestine
RIVER NILE
Egypt
RED SEA
Nubia

2575-2134 BC OLD KINGDOM
2134-2040 BC 9TH TO 11TH DYNASTIES
850 BC GREECE EMERGES FROM DARK AGES
3000-2575 BC EARLY DYNASTIC PERIOD
2040-1640 BC MIDDLE KINGDOM
1550-1070 BC NEW KINGDOM
2485 BC GREAT PYRAMID AT GIZA CONSTRUCTED
1640-1550 BC RULE BY HYKSOS
1070-712 BC LATE DYNASTIC PERIOD

EGYPT

3000 BC   2500 BC   2000 BC   1500 BC   1000 BC

Until 332 BC, ancient Egypt was ruled by 30 families of pharaohs, called dynasties. However, the pharaohs often lost their power to foreign invaders.

Ancient Egypt's history is divided into three main periods. The first is known as the Old Kingdom (2575-2134 BC). During this time, the great pyramids were built as tombs for rulers such as Khufu and Khafre. Next came the Middle Kingdom (2040-1640 BC), a time when trade flourished and the Fayum region was made more suitable for farming. Then, after nearly a hundred years of rule by foreign kings called the Hyksos, there was the New Kingdom (1550-1070 BC).

Under the rule of powerful pharaohs like Thutmose I and Ramesses II, and the weaker boy-king Tutankhamun, New Kingdom Egypt was at its wealthiest. The memorial temple of Amenhotep III was described as:

'*...a monument of eternity and everlastingness, of fine sandstone worked with gold throughout... [with] pavements made of pure silver, all its doors with fine gold.*'

Finally, Egyptian power declined, and the country was conquered by Alexander the Great of Macedonia in 332 BC.

This scene shows one of the huge pyramids under construction by hundreds of workers. The pyramids were tombs for the pharaohs of Old Kingdom Egypt.

753 BC FOUNDATION OF ROME   332 BC EGYPT CONQUERED BY ALEXANDER THE GREAT   AD 780 FIRST MAJOR VIKING RAIDS   AD 1250-1521 AZTECS IN MEXICO

GREECE   140 BC GREECE FALLS   TO ROME   AD 476 ROME FALLS   AD 1070 END OF VIKING AGE   AD 1517 BEGINNING OF REFORMATION

ROMANS   MIDDLE AGES

VIKINGS   AZTECS

500 BC   0   AD 500   AD 1000   AD 1500

5

HISTORY IN EVIDENCE

The civilization of the ancient Egyptians existed many thousands of years ago. So how do we know so much about how they lived and what they did? After the pharaohs, Egypt was ruled by the Greeks and the Romans. Later still, people began to forget about the ancient Egyptians. It was not until the 17th century that archaeologists began to study the great ruins in the desert. Soon they uncovered temples and tombs, and rediscovered the complex lives of the ancient Egyptians.

The most famous site ever found is the tomb of the pharaoh Tutankhamun, who ruled in about 1330 BC. He was buried underground in a place known as the Valley of the Kings (see page 28). Howard Carter, who discovered the tomb in 1922, said his first sight of the treasure was of 'strange animals, statues and gold, everywhere the glint of gold'.

The Rosetta stone dates from 196 BC. On the stone (left) is writing in two Egyptian scripts – hieroglyphic (top) and demotic (centre) – and Greek (bottom). Royal names written in Greek were used by a French scholar named Jean-François Champollion to unravel the meaning of the language of the ancient Egyptians.

Many tombs were decorated with wall paintings, like this one of geese being counted for a 'scribe and counter of grain' named Nebamun. Pharaohs' tombs usually had religious scenes, while other people had scenes of daily life.

Archaeologists use a variety of tools in their work, including buckets, trowels, hoes and brushes for moving soil, to plumb lines, measures, charts and computers for recording and analysing the sites and artefacts they find.

The ancient Egyptians wrote with ink upon papyrus, a grass that grows along the banks of the River Nile. The stems were cut into slices, then pressed together to make long sheets. Many sheets, called scrolls, have survived. This one, from circa 1100 BC, is a report about tomb robberies in Thebes.

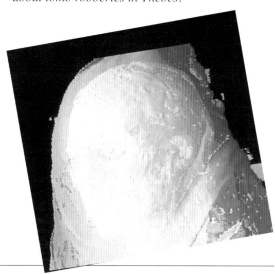

Scientists use special scanners to see inside a mummy without disturbing the fragile body. Computers can then create a 3-D image (right) from the flat pictures.

Buildings reflect the rich history of Egypt – from ancient Egyptian houses (bottom) and Greek and Roman buildings, to forts and mosques (churches) of the Islamic period, and Western-style office blocks.

X-rays are used to study the remains of bodies. The skeletons show us that some pharaohs suffered from hereditary disorders and even that the pharaoh Siptah had polio.

Carter later described his feelings as:
'The day of days, the most wonderful that I have ever lived through and certainly one whose like I can never hope to see again.'

Carter felt like this because he had uncovered so much evidence about how the Egyptians lived. Many more artefacts and some burials of priceless treasure and preserved bodies (called mummies) have also been found: this book shows some of the evidence for the ancient Egyptians' way of life.

The study of sites in Egypt can be hot and sandy work. Many tombs were used in later years as shelters and stables, and have been damaged by the people and animals who lived in them. Very few have been discovered intact.

A WEALTHY FAMILY

New Kingdom 1400 BC

The wealthiest people in Egypt were government officials, landowners, noblemen and priests. They could afford large houses with several rooms, where they lived in comfort with their families.

We know that many families were quite large. People married when they were young: boys at about 14, girls at 12 or even younger. There might be many children and several generations of the same family living in a house.

The scene on the right shows a wealthy couple dressed for a special occasion. Around them are the family's children, the youngest of whom do not wear clothes. They are watching two young men playing a board game called senet.

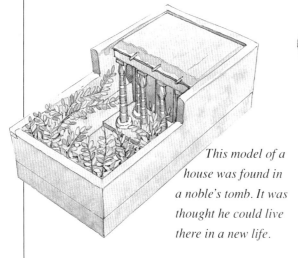

This model of a house was found in a noble's tomb. It was thought he could live there in a new life.

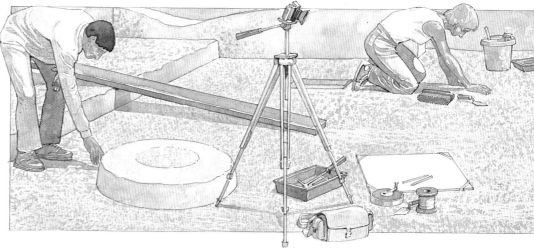

The lady of the house has a cone of scented wax on her head, which will act like a perfume. Wealthy women in particular took great care with their appearance. They wore make-up on their faces and wigs made of human hair, styled in the latest fashions. Wealthy women also owned the furnishings in the house.

This family has many beautiful belongings. Its furniture, such as chairs and tables, is carved out of wood, and the family can afford to wear elaborate pieces of jewellery made of gold and silver. The family will be thankful to the gods for their good fortune. Perhaps they will have a small statue of the god Bes in their house (see page 18).

Among Merit's own belongings were these hair pins and wig (left) and comb and tweezers (bottom). Her wig, which was made of human hair, was found placed neatly on a wooden stand. She would have worn a necklace like the one below.

There were many clothes and textiles in Merit and Kha's tomb, like this woven rug (above left). Merit's folded dressing gown (below) was stored in a woven basket.

Several wall paintings show the Egyptians enjoying senet. This game (left) was played with counters on a squared board, using throwsticks to decide the number of moves made.

Excavations (above) can tell us much about a wealthy family's house. It had spacious rooms, with thick walls to keep out the heat, and wooden pillars to support the roof.

The reconstruction on the right shows a noblewoman named Merit. She was married to a man named Kha. Their tomb has been found intact with many beautiful ornaments.

This ornate wooden chest was for holding glass and stone jars. These would have contained scented oils, creams and kohl. Kohl was a cosmetic used to emphasise the eyes.

FARMING

THE NILE 1200 BC

The Egyptians depended on the fertile soil alongside the Nile for their food. All peasant farmers had to work on their master's estate, but they were also allowed to rent or buy their own land. In the scene on the right we can see workers busily harvesting a crop of barley.

Farmers grew barley and emmer for making bread and brewing a sort of beer, and flax, which was used for making linen cloth. Later, in Roman times, some of Egypt's grain was taken to feed the population of Rome. Fruit and vegetables could also be grown in the warm climate, so even poor people might be able to eat a healthy diet.

Butchers, bakers and brewers are busy at work in this tomb model (above). Some special animals, like the calf below, were mummified.

The unusual tool pictured above right is a cattle brand made of bronze. It was used to mark cattle to show who owned them. The wooden and bronze model above shows what an Egyptian plough looked like. Ploughs were pulled by oxen.

The life of a farmer was long and hard:
> *'He spends the day cutting tools, the night-time twisting ropes. His midday hours he spends working.'*

To water the land, the Egyptians dug irrigation channels. Water could be lifted into these ditches using a simple device called a shaduf, shown standing on the river bank.
When the Nile did not flood, less land could be watered and there might be a famine. In bad years, thousands of people would starve. Farming had its dangers, too. Unwary farmers could lose cattle to the crocodiles that lived in the river. Sometimes people were attacked, so women kept away from the river and men had to wash the clothes.

Farmers used many simple tools during the year. Above right is a hoe; right are a winnowing fan, rake and sickle. The sickle has an edge of sharpened ivory. Winnowing fans were used to toss wheat into the air so that the lighter chaff was separated from the heavier grain.

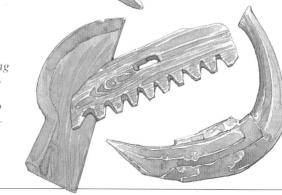

This painted wooden tomb model, from about 1900 BC, shows a servant making bread. He is rolling dough on a stone.

On the right is one of many tomb paintings that show aspects of the farming year.

The land where the Nile flooded its banks was known as the Black Land, because of the colour of the soil. The sandy desert was known as the Red Land.

Farmers kept cattle for their meat and milk. They improved their diet with wild fowl (see page 16), here being cooked over an open fire.

A WORKER'S HOUSE

WESTERN THEBES 1320 BC

Most people could not afford to live like the priests and officials. Many were craftsmen who had to labour long hours making goods for the temple or to barter for food. They lived in simpler houses in towns or villages, like the leatherworker's house shown in the main scene.

Unlike temples and pyramids, which were built of stone, houses were made of mud bricks (see page 22). Over the years these mud-brick houses have been broken up by people, who used the mud as fertilizer for their fields.

As towns grew, house after house was built right next to each other. Some houses were two storeys high, and had several rooms and a cellar.

Many dolls have been found in Egyptian tombs. This one, made of wood, has movable arms. She is also wearing earrings!

Craftsmen could make or afford to buy simple toys for their children, like this toy mouse and spinning top and stick (right).

In the scene above we can see a leatherworker's family in their house. After work the family would gather for a simple meal (left). The boy has a side lock of hair, which was a symbol of youth: when he is older it will be cut off.

12

The front of a typical house faced straight onto the street – there were no grassy front gardens! At the back there was a small kitchen yard with an oven. Archaeological evidence shows that the walls of a house were usually plastered and then painted white. The windows were quite small, to keep out the heat, and the inside walls might be painted and decorated. Each house had steps leading to a flat roof, where the family could gather and catch the cool evening breeze.

Most craftsmen worked at the temples (see page 20). Around the temple courtyards there were separate workshops for goldsmiths and silver-smiths, glass blowers, metalworkers, potters, masons, carpenters and leatherworkers. Some worked from their own homes – perhaps the leather-worker in the scene is making things for his family or friends.

Bread was a major part of a family's diet. The triangular loaf (above left), called ta, is 3,500 years old! The strainer and sieve (above) were used for straining beer before it was drunk.

This dig (left) shows archaeologists at work in the town of Deir el-Medina, built in about 1500 BC. It housed the families of craftsmen working in the Valley of the Kings, where many royal tombs were sited. Because the town was in the desert, more of the buildings has been preserved. Some had walls on foundations made of stone.

Above and right are a typical leather sandal and a wooden stool covered in plaited leather. The woven rush basket (far right) would have held the worker's tools.

TRADE

THE NILE 1460 BC

The Egyptians became very wealthy through trade. There were very few roads, because the Nile floods washed them away! Therefore people often travelled on the river in small boats. These were made out of reeds, because wood was scarce in a land where trees rarely grew.

Although reed boats were quite strong, they could not carry heavy loads or travel on the open sea. Instead, the pharaohs and wealthy merchants made stronger ships of wood. In the scene, exotic goods, such as ivory, animal furs and even a baby giraffe, are being unloaded from a large sea-going ship. It has probably just returned from a trading expedition to one of the African lands to the south. In about 1470 BC, a fleet of ships was sent by Queen Hatshepsut to trade with the Land of Punt (the country we know as Somalia). In the reliefs on the right we can see Hatshepsut's ships and sailors.

Some of the best evidence of trade is shown by these reliefs of Hatshepsut's ships from her temple at Deir el-Bahari. On the left, sailors are working in the rigging while others row the ship. On the right, amphorae and incense trees in pots are being carried on board ship as a baboon looks on.

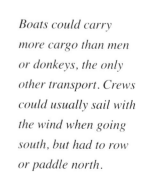

Thirty-five model boats were found in Tutankhamun's tomb. This one has two large steering oars and a cabin for an important passenger.

Boats could carry more cargo than men or donkeys, the only other transport. Crews could usually sail with the wind when going south, but had to row or paddle north.

This beautiful dish was used to spoon cosmetics. It is made from ivory (elephant or hippo tusks), which probably came from Nubia or even further south.

These jars and amphorae were used to store and carry goods such as wine or grain. The pottery, often made from mud from the Nile, kept the contents cool. Each jar was capped with a cloth plug sealed with clay or wax.

Blue-painted amphora, c1330 BC

Large jar, c2850 BC

Small jar, c2100 BC

Wine jar, c1330 BC

Thousands of glassware jars and pots (left) were produced during the 18th dynasty. Many objects, like this tile (above left), were made of ground quartz which was glazed to give a glassy appearance. The Egyptians were also experts at making stone pots and jars (above), including the pot in the shape of a bird.

We know that the Egyptians traded in the Mediterranean and with other parts of Africa. Traders swapped grain, gold, linen and papyrus for metals such as copper and silver, Greek olive oil, incense from Punt and Arabia, and wood from the eastern Mediterranean for making boats and furniture.

The Egyptians did not use coins until about 300 BC. Before this they had a successful system of swapping goods, called bartering. For example, the sailors of the pharaoh's navy were paid in sacks of grain, which they bartered for the things they needed. Everyone knew the value of items: a sack of grain was worth one pottery dish and a duck!

HUNTING AND FISHING

THE NILE 1400 BC

Along the Nile, and in the marshy areas near the sea, the Egyptians fished from boats and hunted ducks, geese and other wild fowl. When the river was in flood they also dug pits and pools, so that fish would be stranded in them when the waters receded.

In the scene on the right, a nobleman and his wife are hunting ducks. He is throwing a curved stick that can kill or stun a bird. Similar 'snake sticks' were found in the tomb of Tutankhamun. Some hunters, like the one in the wall painting below, used tame ducks to lure other birds to their boat. They also trained cats to retrieve the birds they hit. Another method of hunting was to lure flocks of birds into large nets strung across the water or between the reeds.

Behind him, the hunter's servants are amusing themselves by fishing. For the wealthy, hunting was an exciting sport. For poorer people who rarely had meat to eat, birds and fish were an important source of protein.

This painting found in the tomb of Nebamun (see page 6) is excellent evidence for how the Egyptians hunted wild fowl.

Fishermen worked together to trap fish in a net slung between their boats. The model on the right is one of many found in the tomb of an official named Meket Re.

Curved throwing sticks and arrows (right) were used to kill wild fowl. Arrows were made from sharpened reeds, tipped with pointed bone or metal.

Wild fowl were also hunted by firing small stones from a sling (above). Metal fish hooks (left) were used to catch fish, while larger prey, such as crocodiles and hippopotamuses, could only be hunted with metal-tipped harpoons.

The fishermen have chased a shoal of small fish into shallow water and trapped them in a net. Large fish were hunted with spears, or were lured to baited sticks and lines, a bit like anglers use a rod or pole to catch fish today.

The wealthy also hunted on dry land. Popular prey included antelope, gazelle and wild cattle. Some wall paintings show leopards, ostriches and lions being hunted from horse-drawn chariots – a lion skin was a great prize!

Sometimes expeditions set out to hunt hippopotamuses and crocodiles, which could be a great danger to boats and farmers' cattle. The male hippo, which is a peaceful animal unless it is disturbed, was believed to represent Seth, the god of evil and wrong-doing.

The Nile was full of fish, including huge perch that weighed over 50 kilograms. This beautiful glass flask was made to hold perfume or ointment.

Fishermen had to be very careful – an angry hippopotamus could easily overturn a light, fragile boat. This model is made of a glassy material known as faience.

17

Procession of the God

Thebes 1250 bc

The Egyptians worshipped many gods and goddesses, such as the sun god, Amun. They believed that everything on Earth had been made by these deities. Many gods were shown with human bodies and the heads of animals or birds.

Many of the deities were associated with aspects of nature, such as the sun and stars, or a particular hill or tree. Some were worshipped at home. People kept small statues of them in shrines in their houses (see page 8), and also wore their images or symbols as small lucky charms.

The main gods and goddesses had their own temples where their spirits lived in gold or stone images. In theory only the pharaoh could look after a deity's image, because the pharaoh was believed to be a living god. In practice, every day the high priest of each temple brought food and burned incense for the image, which was kept in a shrine at the heart of the temple.

Above is the top from a standard which was used in ceremonial processions. The falcon represents the god Horus, son of the god Osiris and the goddess Isis. The pharaoh was believed to be Horus on Earth.

The goddess Bastet, shown below in the form of a cat, was thought to be the daughter of the sun god Re. She was believed to help ripen the corn, and make crops grow.

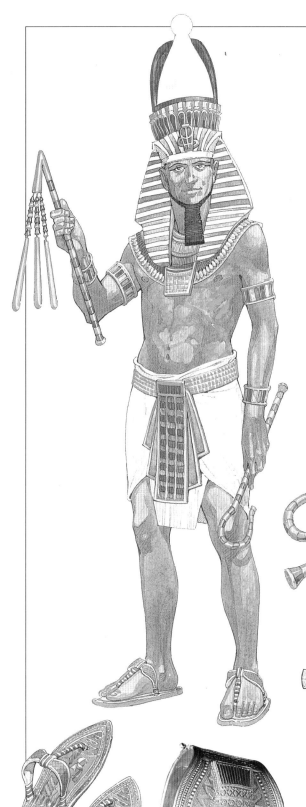

As the living Horus, the pharaoh (top) was responsible for defending Egypt. The sandals above belonged to Tutankhamun. Pictured on the soles are the pharaoh's enemies, whom he symbolically trod underfoot. The golden bracelet probably belonged to Ramesses II.

The crook and flail (top) were emblems of Osiris, the god of the dead. They were used by the pharaoh on ceremonial occasions. The ankh (above) was the hieroglyph for life. Ankhs were popular as lucky charms and were often worn as jewellery.

Above and right are statuettes of the gods Bes and Khnum. The ugly Bes (above) was worshipped as a god of the family and newborn children. Khnum was a god of the Nile, who ordered it to flood each year.

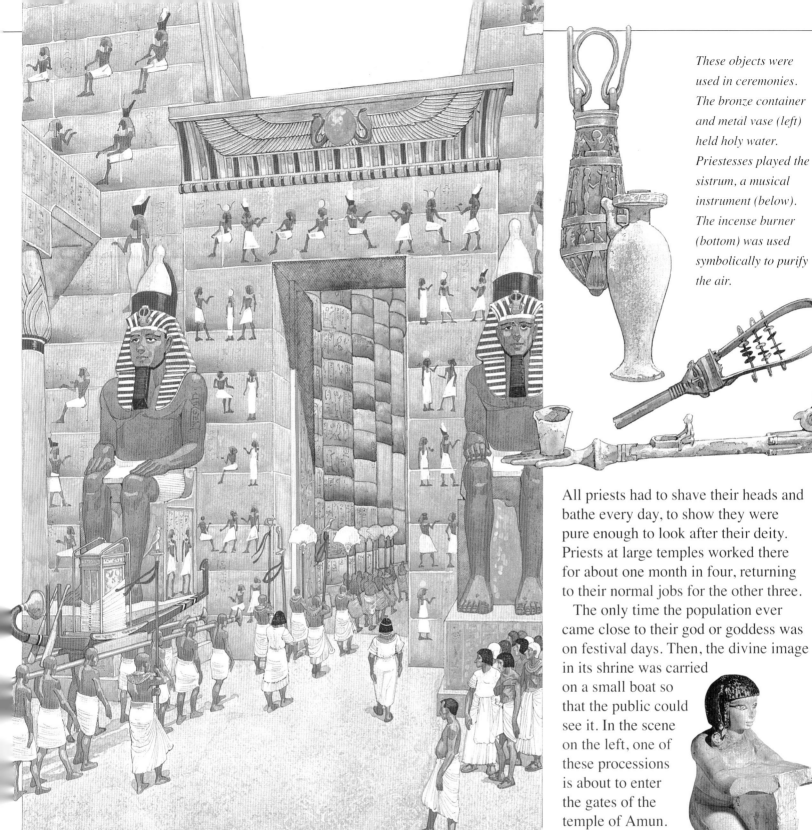

These objects were used in ceremonies. The bronze container and metal vase (left) held holy water. Priestesses played the sistrum, a musical instrument (below). The incense burner (bottom) was used symbolically to purify the air.

All priests had to shave their heads and bathe every day, to show they were pure enough to look after their deity. Priests at large temples worked there for about one month in four, returning to their normal jobs for the other three.

The only time the population ever came close to their god or goddess was on festival days. Then, the divine image in its shrine was carried on a small boat so that the public could see it. In the scene on the left, one of these processions is about to enter the gates of the temple of Amun.

The southern temple to Amun at Thebes, now called Luxor, was built by Amenhotep III. Ramesses II added six statues of himself. Each year, Amun's image was brought here from the northern temple at Karnak.

This statue shows a priest offering food to his deity. Important people were allowed to put statues of themselves in temples so they could stay close to their deity.

LIFE AT THE TEMPLE

The largest temples were a complex network of buildings. Many, like those at Karnak and Luxor, had colossal statues that guarded their gateways, and vast courtyards. The innermost shrine of the deity was reached by passing through columned halls.

Most temples were very wealthy. The pharaohs gave them huge estates and booty from wars, to thank the deities for their aid. And each temple also received taxes from people living on its lands, which were paid in goods such as grain, gold, beer and wine. In turn, these were used to pay the people who worked in the temple.

Therefore, as well as the musicians, cooks and craftsmen who prepared offerings for the deity, the temples employed many officials to administer the taxes and storehouses. At the time of Ramesses III, the temples and estates of the god Amun had a quarter of a million hectares of land in Thebes and employed over 80,000 workers!

The unit of weight was the deben, divided into 10 kite. These weights were used to give a value to goods. Below are round 1, 2 and 5 kite and a 4 deben weight. The wealthy could pay for porters (right) to carry their goods.

This rush chest (right) was a doctor's dispensing case for carrying medicines and ointments. People also wore amulets (below) to protect themselves from illness and to ward off evil spirits.

Many temples have not survived, because pharaohs often took stone from older buildings to construct new ones. In Thebes, archaeologists have found the remains of the granaries at Ramesses II's own memorial temple, the Ramesseum. It was important to store grain when it was plentiful, in case there was a famine.

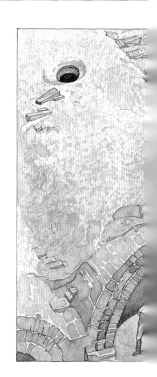

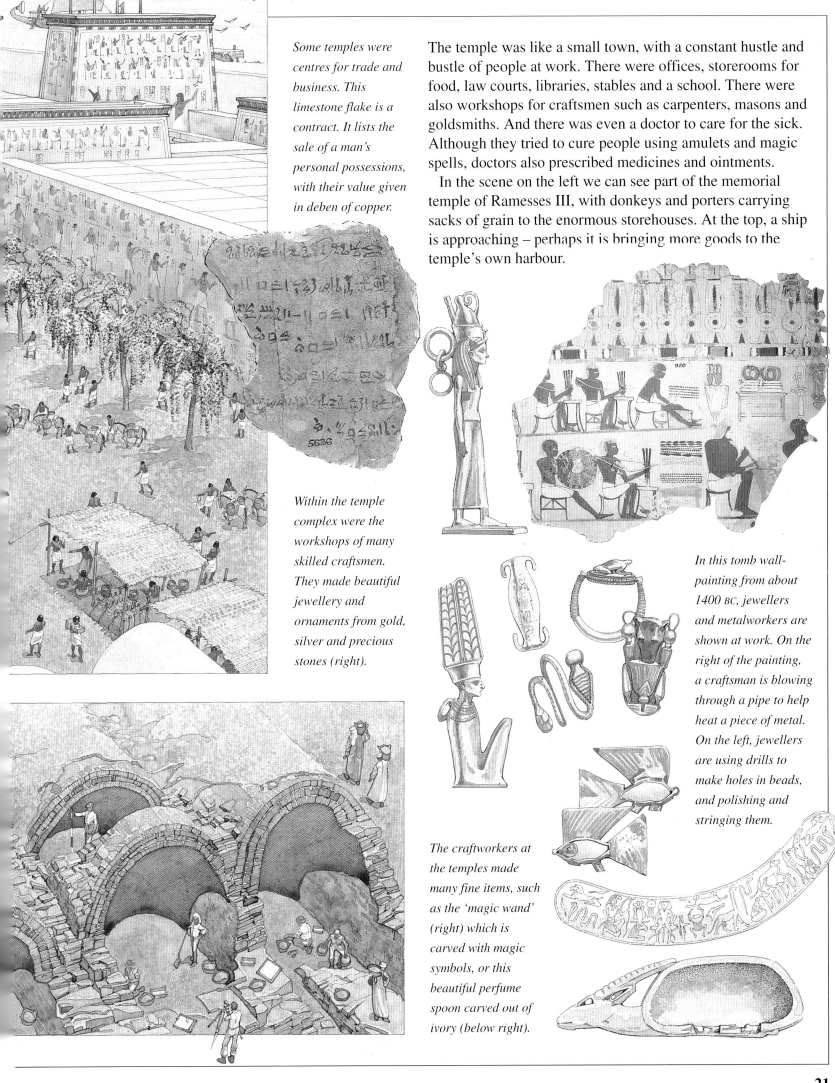

Some temples were centres for trade and business. This limestone flake is a contract. It lists the sale of a man's personal possessions, with their value given in deben of copper.

The temple was like a small town, with a constant hustle and bustle of people at work. There were offices, storerooms for food, law courts, libraries, stables and a school. There were also workshops for craftsmen such as carpenters, masons and goldsmiths. And there was even a doctor to care for the sick. Although they tried to cure people using amulets and magic spells, doctors also prescribed medicines and ointments.

In the scene on the left we can see part of the memorial temple of Ramesses III, with donkeys and porters carrying sacks of grain to the enormous storehouses. At the top, a ship is approaching – perhaps it is bringing more goods to the temple's own harbour.

Within the temple complex were the workshops of many skilled craftsmen. They made beautiful jewellery and ornaments from gold, silver and precious stones (right).

In this tomb wall-painting from about 1400 BC, jewellers and metalworkers are shown at work. On the right of the painting, a craftsman is blowing through a pipe to help heat a piece of metal. On the left, jewellers are using drills to make holes in beads, and polishing and stringing them.

The craftworkers at the temples made many fine items, such as the 'magic wand' (right) which is carved with magic symbols, or this beautiful perfume spoon carved out of ivory (below right).

MOVING A COLOSSUS

THEBES CIRCA 1360 BC

Egypt is famous for its huge monuments. As well as the towering pyramids (see page 4), there were many extensive temples and large statues. In the scene on the right, workers are dragging one of two enormous stone statues, now known as the Colossi of Memnon, to the memorial temple of the pharaoh Amenhotep III.

No-one can be certain how the pyramids were built, but we do know more about the Colossi. Amenhotep had these huge statues made to please the gods and to show that he, too, had power. The statues were carved in quarries far to the south of Thebes. They were then taken up the Nile by boat, before being dragged across land on sledges and wooden rollers. It must have been very tiring work!

Soldiers were given wooden ration tokens (above) as a method of payment. The men could exchange these tokens for food.

The Egyptians built monuments with great precision, using tools like this hammer, plumb line (for checking that stones were standing straight) and a cubit measure. The cubit was 52.5 cm long.

Other tools found include chisels, a mallet and a brick mould. Bricks were made by mixing mud and straw then pressing them into the mould. The mixture was left to bake in the sun until it hardened.

So who built the monuments? The Colossi of Memnon were carved by skilled stone workers, experts at their craft. However, the statues were moved by soldiers. Egypt was not at war, so the pharaoh wanted to keep his troops busy.

Most monuments, including the pyramids, were probably built by ordinary men who farmed the land for most of the year. When the Nile flooded its banks, the pharaoh employed them to do the heavy work. We know that they had to report for work each day and that they were paid a small wage in goods. Archaeologists have even found written evidence of workers going on strike until they were paid!

'It is because of hunger and because of thirst that we come here. There is no clothing, no ointment [for dry skin], no fish, no vegetables. Send to pharaoh, our good lord, about it. And send to the vizier, our superior, that sustenance be made for us.'

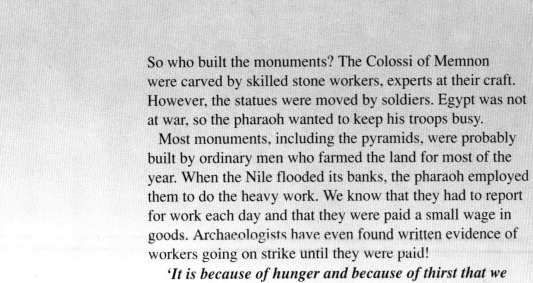

The writing on this piece of limestone is an attendance record for workers in the Valley of the Kings.

This papyrus scroll shows calculations of the height and angles of pyramids. It was used to train the men who would be in charge of building monuments.

In 1798, Napoleon's army invaded Egypt. It was accompanied by many scholars and artists who studied Egypt's ancient sites, including the Colossi. They made detailed records of all the artefacts they found.

On the right is part of a huge sandstone statue of the pharaoh Akhenaten, the son of Amenhotep III. He built a new city, called Akhetaten, with a magnificent new temple, to replace Thebes as the capital.

SCRIBES

MEMPHIS 2500 BC

The pharaoh ruled with the aid of many officials and scribes. They ran the country, recording how much trade was done and collecting taxes. Everyone had to pay taxes, so scribes took details of people's wealth and calculated how much they had to pay.

Boys needed a good education to become a scribe. So people tried to send their sons to school – girls stayed at home to help look after the house. Most poor children went to a local village school, but some went to school at the temples, with the sons of nobles and officials. There they learned to read and write, some basic mathematics and simple record-keeping. Able boys, whose parents could afford it, were sent to study more advanced subjects, such as astronomy and geography.

Discipline was hard. In the scene on the right a trainee scribe is being beaten for not doing his work properly:

'O scribe do not be idle, or you will be cursed. Do not give your heart to pleasure or you will fail. Do not spend a day in idleness or you will be beaten. A boy's ear is on his back side and he listens when he is beaten.'

Schoolboys and trainee scribes practised writing on pieces of stone or pottery, called ostraca.

The symbol below is the hieroglyph for a scribe. It shows (from left to right) a brush holder, water pot and a palette for mixing pigments. Alongside it is an inscribed tag used to label scrolls. Scribes could then tell at a glance which scroll they needed without having to unroll them all.

Scribes were the civil servants of the ancient Egyptian state. High officials were allowed to use seals (left) with the name and titles of the king, to show they had his authority.

Many officials had statues showing them as scribes, with an open papyrus scroll in their lap (below). They wanted every- body to know how educated and important they were.

The maker of this tomb model of a granary included scribes busily recording the amount of grain being stored.

Many examples of scribes' work have survived. The early Egyptians wrote using hieroglyphs. These were pictures used to represent sounds or groups of sounds. The whole alphabet consisted of over 700 hieroglyphs.

Hieroglyphs were mainly used on buildings and for religious texts. For everyday use, scribes developed hieratic script. This was usually written in black and red ink with a brush or sharpened reed. In later times, an even simpler script, called demotic, came into use.

The stone carving below shows a group of scribes who seem to be bowing to their master. Each has a papyrus scroll, like the one on the right which records a loan of wheat and barley.

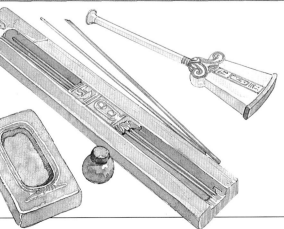

A scribe's tools included a palette and water pot for mixing colours, another for his pens and red and black inks, fine reed pens, and a tool for smoothing papyrus.

WARFARE

SYRIA 1274 BC

Egypt was protected from other countries by the desert and the sea. However, its borders were attacked by enemies such as the Assyrians, the Hittites and the Sea People. On these occasions, the pharaoh led his men into battle.

Most Egyptian soldiers fought on foot. They carried long spears with metal tips, and slings, daggers or curved swords. Some were archers, armed with strong wooden and metal-tipped arrows. Few wore any armour, but many carried shields.

The pharaoh went to war in a wooden chariot pulled by two horses. Chariots had a crew of two – a driver and an archer, who could fire his bow as the chariot raced across the desert.

The pharaoh had his weapons made by the finest craftsmen. These two magnificent iron daggers, with decorated gold handles, had been placed in the pharaoh Tutankhamun's tomb (see page 28).

Most Egyptian soldiers (left) carried a sword and shield. Their only other protection was a white linen skirt and a simple headdress to keep off the hot sun. Some weapons found include arrow heads, a curved sword (a khepesh), an axe and this long bronze stabbing sword.

Many types of soldier fought in the Egyptian army. The tomb model below shows a company of spearmen.

Many reliefs picture prisoners taken in battle. They were always shown with their hands bound, as on these tiles from the reign of Ramesses III.

Ramesses II had the story of his exploits at Qadesh told on many temples (above), including those at Abu Simbel, Karnak and Luxor, as well as his memorial temple!

In the main scene we can see the Battle of Qadesh, fought by Ramesses II and his army. Ramesses was accompanied into battle by his pet lion, which is bounding beside his chariot! We know about the battle because Ramesses had picture carvings of it on his temples, and also had an account written. At one point Ramesses said he was surrounded by the Hittites: 'I call upon thee, my father Amun, for I am in the midst of a multitude of foes.' Inspired, Ramesses charged the enemy in his chariot and won a great victory:

'All about him was the heat of fire... He was mighty, his heart stout.'

Sometimes, prisoners of war were captured and brought back to Egypt as slaves. The Egyptians also attacked and conquered countries for their natural resources. For example, they invaded the neighbouring country of Nubia so they could take gold from the Nubian mines.

Most of our evidence about Egyptian chariots comes from stone carvings, and this example that was found in the tomb of the young pharaoh Tutankhamun.

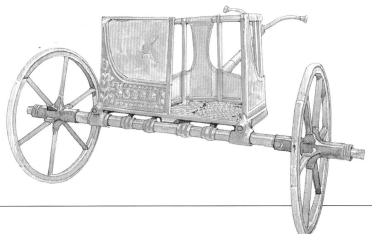

THE TOMB OF TUTANKHAMUN

VALLEY OF THE KINGS CIRCA 1320 BC

The discovery of the tomb of Tutankhamun in the Valley of the Kings in 1922 is one of the most famous archaeological finds. Yet the tomb's fabulous treasures and the king's body were put there in a hurry, because he had died when just 18 years of age.

Tutankhamun had not been a strong or popular king, and some historians believe he was murdered. Suddenly, everyone had to prepare for his funeral.

People believed a person's soul needed a body or it would perish. So the body's internal organs were removed and placed in containers called canopic jars. The body was then preserved as a mummy.

This pottery mask was worn by a priest playing the part of Anubis, the god of the dead. Models of the jackal-headed Anubis were put in tombs to guard the bodies placed there.

Left are some of the items used during the 'Opening of the Mouth' ceremony. The trumpet was also found in the tomb. It was probably used during hunts.

The tomb was packed with hundreds of items, each of which was studied and recorded. Here we can see Howard Carter carefully removing the king's outer coffin from the middle coffin.

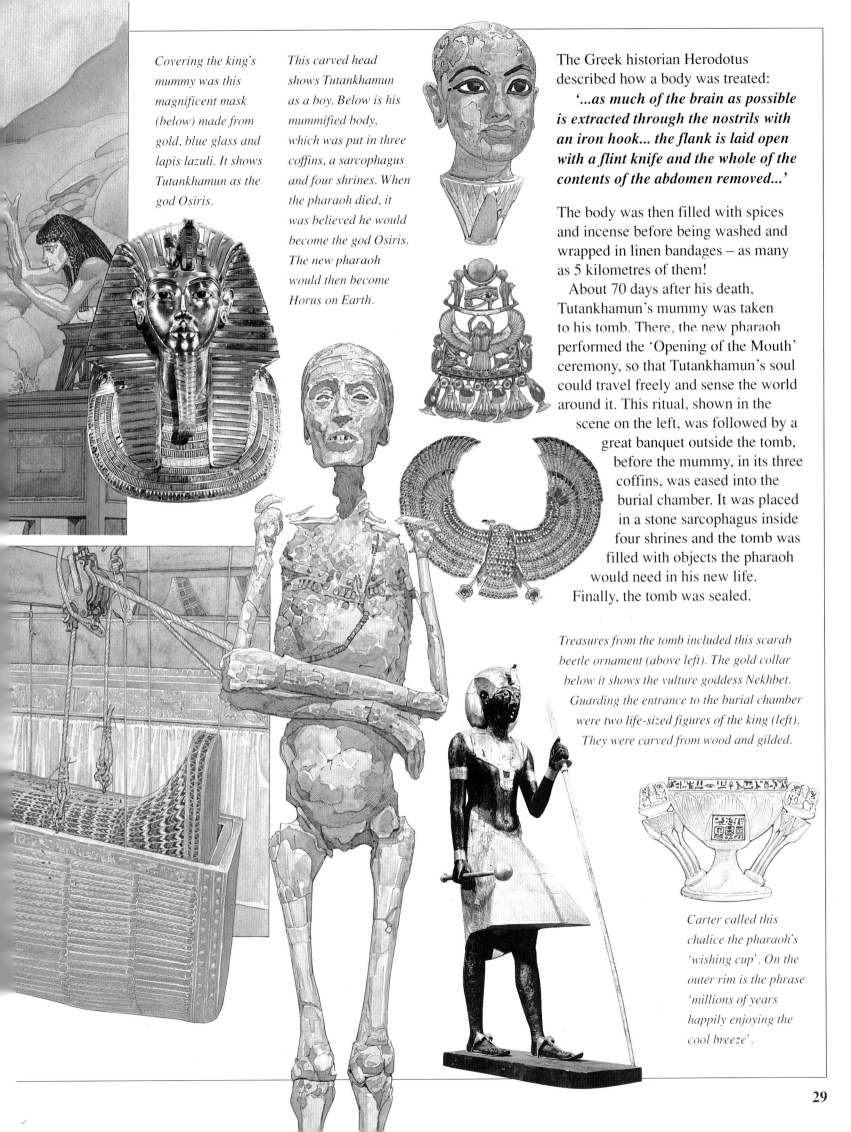

Covering the king's mummy was this magnificent mask (below) made from gold, blue glass and lapis lazuli. It shows Tutankhamun as the god Osiris.

This carved head shows Tutankhamun as a boy. Below is his mummified body, which was put in three coffins, a sarcophagus and four shrines. When the pharaoh died, it was believed he would become the god Osiris. The new pharaoh would then become Horus on Earth.

The Greek historian Herodotus described how a body was treated:

'...as much of the brain as possible is extracted through the nostrils with an iron hook... the flank is laid open with a flint knife and the whole of the contents of the abdomen removed...'

The body was then filled with spices and incense before being washed and wrapped in linen bandages – as many as 5 kilometres of them!

About 70 days after his death, Tutankhamun's mummy was taken to his tomb. There, the new pharaoh performed the 'Opening of the Mouth' ceremony, so that Tutankhamun's soul could travel freely and sense the world around it. This ritual, shown in the scene on the left, was followed by a great banquet outside the tomb, before the mummy, in its three coffins, was eased into the burial chamber. It was placed in a stone sarcophagus inside four shrines and the tomb was filled with objects the pharaoh would need in his new life. Finally, the tomb was sealed.

Treasures from the tomb included this scarab beetle ornament (above left). The gold collar below it shows the vulture goddess Nekhbet. Guarding the entrance to the burial chamber were two life-sized figures of the king (left). They were carved from wood and gilded.

Carter called this chalice the pharaoh's 'wishing cup'. On the outer rim is the phrase 'millions of years happily enjoying the cool breeze'.

GLOSSARY

This list explains the meaning of some of the words
and terms used in the book.

**AMPHORA
AND JAR**

AMPHORA   Usually, a two-handled jar or container.

AMULET   A small charm or piece of jewellery worn as protection
against evil.

AMUN   The sun god, who became chief god of Egypt.

ANKH   A hieroglyph which represented life.

ARTEFACT   An object from the past that has been made by people.

BARTER   To exchange goods for something other than money.

COLOSSI   Enormous statues. The Colossi of Memnon were named
after one had been damaged in an earthquake in 27 BC.
Each morning, as the statue warmed up, the stone made
popping and creaking noises. People thought that the statue
was singing, and so named both after Memnon, the son of
the goddess of the dawn, Aurora.

ANKH

DEBEN   A unit of weight, about 90 grams, used to give a value to
goods being bartered. There were 10 kite in a deben.

DEITY   A god or goddess.

DELTA   The marshy land of Lower Egypt, where the ancient Nile
divided into about 12 main channels.

DEMOTIC   An Egyptian script, written using ink on papyrus or pottery.

DYNASTY   A group of pharaohs who ruled after one another.

EMMER   A type of grain, an early form of wheat.

GILDED   Something which has been covered with a thin layer of
gold leaf.

HIERATIC   An Egyptian script, written using ink on papyrus or pottery.

HIEROGLYPHS   The symbols which made up the picture writing of the
ancient Egyptians.

HIEROGLYPHS ON A SCROLL TAG

HORUS   God of kingship and protector of the pharaoh.

ISIS   Goddess of magic, wife of Osiris and mother of Horus.

IVORY   The tusks of an elephant or hippopotamus.

LAPIS LAZULI   A semi-precious stone that is dark blue in colour.

MUMMY   A preserved body. Priests called embalmers used the
natural chemical natron to stop the body rotting.

OSIRIS   Lord of the Underworld, husband of Isis, father of Horus.

PALETTE   A board on which colours or inks are mixed.

PHARAOH   The title given to the kings of ancient Egypt. The Egyptian
word originally meant 'great house' and referred to the
king's palace. Later it was used to describe the king himself.

IVORY SPOON

PIGMENT   A powder which is mixed with water to make a paint.

PRIEST   An important official in a temple. Female priests are called
priestesses. The pharaoh was the most important priest.

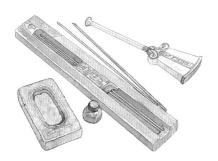

PALETTE AND OTHER SCRIBE'S TOOLS

SARCOPHAGUS	A large outer coffin, usually decorated.
SHRINE	A tomb or place that is important to religious people.
TOMB	The burial place of a dead person. Early tombs, such as the pyramids, were above ground. Later, most people were buried underground.
TOMB MODEL	A model placed in a tomb. It was believed the model would work for a person in a new life after death.
VALLEY OF THE KINGS	A remote valley in the desert where many pharaohs were buried in underground tombs.

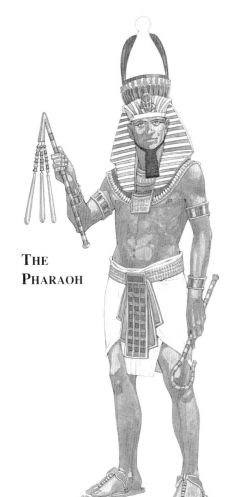

THE PHARAOH

KEY DATES

circa 3000 BC	King Narmer unites Upper and Lower Egypt.
2920-2575	1st to 3rd dynasties. Invasions of Nubia. Memphis is the capital city.
2575-2134	4th to 8th dynasties. Old Kingdom. The pyramids are built for rulers like Khufu and Khafre. The sun-god Re is the most important deity.
2134-2040	9th to 11th dynasties. A time of famine and foreign invasions. Egypt is controlled mainly by local rulers.
2040-1640	11th to 14th dynasties. Middle Kingdom. At Thebes, temples are built to Amun, the new chief god, and Osiris is worshipped widely.
1640-1550	15th to 17th dynasties. Egypt is ruled by the Hyksos, who introduce chariots and the use of bronze.
1550-1070	18th to 20th dynasties. New Kingdom. Capital moved to Thebes.
1473-1458	Queen Hatshepsut (18th dynasty) reigns as pharaoh. Trading expedition to the Land of Punt.
1391-1353	Amenhotep III (18th dynasty) reigns as pharaoh. Building of the Colossi of Memnon and a new temple to Amun at Luxor.
1333-1320	The young Tutankhamun (18th dynasty) reigns as pharaoh.
1290-1224	Ramesses II (19th dynasty) reigns as pharaoh. Battle of Qadesh and the building of his memorial temple.
1070-712	21st to 25th dynasties.
712-332	Egypt ruled mainly by Nubians, Assyrians and Persians.
332	Egypt conquered by Alexander the Great, who founds the city of Alexandria. Rule by Greek kings and, later, the Romans.
47-30 BC	Cleopatra reigns as Queen of Egypt, under Roman protection.
30 BC	Egypt becomes a Roman colony.

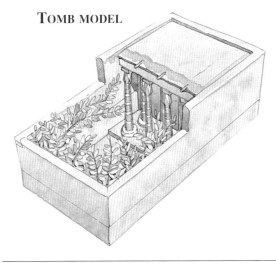

TOMB MODEL

QUOTATIONS

The description of Amenhotep's temple survives on a carved column. Howard Carter's discovery was the greatest achievement of his long but difficult career. He spent 10 years recording thoroughly and conserving the objects that he had found. The quotations on farming and a scribe's life were written by a teacher to persuade his pupils that a scribe had the best job. The petition of workers has survived on an ostracon, a limestone flake. It dates from about 1160 BC. The description of Ramesses II's 'victory' at Qadesh comes from a poem from his reign. Herodotus wrote about mummification in the fifth century BC, but we know the practice had changed little since Tutankhamun's time.

INDEX

Akhetaten 23
Alexander the Great 5
Amenhotep III 5, 19, 22
amphorae 14, 15, 30
amulets 20, 21, 30
Amun 18, 19, 20, 27, 30
ankhs 18, 30
Anubis 28
archaeological discoveries 6, 7
archaeological tools and equipment 6
architecture 7

Bartering 15, 30
Bastet 18
beer 10, 13
Bes 8, 18
breadmaking 11
bricks 12, 22
building materials 12

Canopic jars 28
Carter, Howard 6, 7, 28
ceremonial objects 18, 19, 28
chariots 26, 27
charms and spells 18, 20, 21
children 8, 12, 24
clothes and textiles 9, 10
coins 15
Colossi of Memnon 22, 23, 30
conquests of Egypt 5, 23
cosmetics 8, 9, 15
craftsmen 12, 13, 20, 21

Deir el-Medina 13
demotic script 5, 25, 30
dynasties 5, 30

Education 24

Family life 8-9, 12-13
farming 5, 10-11, 18
fashion and style 8, 9
festivals 19
flooding 4, 10, 11, 14, 16, 18, 23
food 10, 11, 13, 16, 20
footwear 13, 18
furnishings 8, 13

Games and pastimes 8, 9
glassware 15, 17
gods and goddesses 8, 17, 18, 19, 28, 29

Hatshepsut, Queen 14
Herodotus 29
hieroglyphs 6, 18, 24, 25, 30
Horus 18, 29, 30
houses 8-9, 12-13
hunting and fishing 16-17
Hyksos 5

Illnesses 7, 20, 21
irrigation 10
Isis 18, 30

Jewellery and ornaments 9, 18, 21, 29

Karnak 19, 20, 27
Khnum 18

Language 6
Luxor see Thebes

Maps
  ancient Egypt 4
  archaeological sites 4
masks 28, 29
medicines 20, 21
merchants 14
Middle Kingdom 5
monuments 22-3
mummies 6, 7, 28, 29, 30
musical instruments 19

New Kingdom 5
Nile 4, 10, 11, 14, 16, 17, 18, 22, 23
nobles 8, 9, 16
Nubia 15, 27

Officials 8, 20, 24
Old Kingdom 5
Opening of the Mouth ceremony 28, 29
Osiris 18, 29, 30

Papyrus 6, 15, 24, 25
pharaohs 4, 5, 7, 14, 18, 20, 23, 24, 26, 30
pottery 15, 28
priests and priestesses 8, 18, 19, 28, 30
pyramids 5, 12, 22, 23

Qadesh, Battle of 27

Ramesses II 5, 18, 19, 20, 27
Rosetta stone 6

Sarcophagus 29, 31
scribes 6, 24-5
scripts 6, 25, 30
scrolls 6, 23, 24, 25
seals 24
senet (board game) 8, 9
ships and boats 14, 15, 16, 17, 19, 21
shrines 8, 18, 19, 31
slaves 27
soldiers 22, 23, 26
statues 8, 18, 19, 22, 23, 24
stone carvings 25, 27

Taxes 20, 24
temples 12, 13, 18, 19, 20-1, 22, 27
Thebes (Luxor) 19, 20, 23, 27
Thutmose I 5
timeline 4-5
tomb models 10, 11, 26, 31
tomb robberies 6
tombs 5, 6, 7, 13, 16, 21, 28-9, 31
  see also pyramids
tools
  archaeological 6
  building 22
  farming 10
toys 12
trade 5, 14-15, 21, 24
Tutankhamun 5, 6, 14, 16, 18, 26, 27, 28-9

Unification of Egypt 4

Valley of the Kings 6, 13, 23, 28, 31

Wall paintings 6, 9, 11, 16, 17, 21
warfare 26-7
weapons 16, 17, 26
weights 20, 30
women 8, 9
writing materials 6, 24, 25